T0148919

ICE HOUSE BOOKS

Published by Ice House Books

Copyright © 2020 Ice House Books

Compiled by Rebecca Du Pontet & Raphaella Thompson
Designed and illustrated by Emily Curtis

Ice House Books is an imprint of Half Moon Bay Limited
The Ice House, 124 Walcot Street, Bath, BA1 5BG
www.icehousebooks.co.uk

ISBN 978-1-912867-75-2

Printed in China

To:

....

From:

....

Contents

Make Your Own
Sugar Syrup

MAKES 340 ML (12 FL OZ)
PREP 10 MINUTES

INGREDIENTS
240 ml (8¼ fl oz) water
200 g (7 oz) caster sugar

METHOD
1. Mix the sugar and water in a medium-sized saucepan.
2. Bring the mixture to the boil, constantly stirring until the sugar has fully dissolved and the liquid has thickened.
3. Allow the sugar syrup to cool completely, then transfer it to a glass container and keep in the fridge for up to one month.
4. Experiment with different flavoured syrups – citrus, ginger, cucumber – take your pick!

On the Rum

SERVES 1 | PREP 5 MINUTES

INGREDIENTS

100 g (3½ oz) pineapple,
chopped
1 shot dark rum
½ shot lime juice
1 tsp coconut sugar
½ tsp ginger, finely grated
ice cubes
mint sprig for garnish

METHOD

1. Put all the ingredients (except
   the mint) in a blender and blend
   until smooth.
2. Pour the mixture into an ice-filled
   glass and garnish with mint.

Rum
Knickerbocker

SERVES 1 | PREP 5 MINUTES

INGREDIENTS

ice cubes
2 shots gold rum
½ shot triple sec
1 shot lime juice
½ shot raspberry syrup
fresh raspberries for garnish

METHOD

1. Add all the ingredients (except the garnish) to an ice-filled cocktail shaker. Put the lid on and shake until the outside is cold and frosty.

2. Pour into a glass filled with crushed ice and garnish with fresh raspberries.

IF RUM CAN'T FIX
IT YOU'RE NOT
USING ENOUGH.

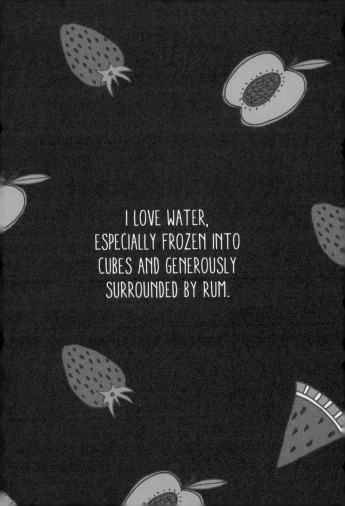

I LOVE WATER,
ESPECIALLY FROZEN INTO
CUBES AND GENEROUSLY
SURROUNDED BY RUM.

(If You Like)
Piña Colada

SERVES 1 | PREP 5 MINUTES

INGREDIENTS

ice cubes
2 shots coconut milk
2 shots gold rum
3 shots pineapple juice
½ shot lime juice
2 tbsp sugar syrup
pineapple slice for garnish

METHOD

1. Put a glass full of ice into a blender and blend until crushed.

2. Stir the coconut milk so it's smooth before adding to the ice.

3. Add the rum, pineapple and lime juice and sugar syrup (to taste) to a blender and blend until smooth.

4. Pour into a glass and garnish with a slice of pineapple.

Pumpkin
Spiced

SERVES 1 | PREP 5 MINUTES

INGREDIENTS

ice cubes
2 shots white rum
2 shots pumpkin purée
1 shot lemonade
orange slice for garnish

METHOD

1. Fill an ice-filled cocktail shaker with all the ingredients (except the orange slice).

2. Put the lid on the shaker and shake until the outside becomes cold and frosty.

3. Strain the mixture into an ice-filled glass, top with lemonade and garnish with the orange slice.

IN THE 18TH CENTURY,
THE ROYAL NAVY SUPPLIED
ITS SAILORS WITH HALF A
PINT OF RUM A DAY.
CHEERS!

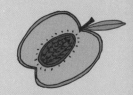

ALL ROADS LEAD TO RUM.

W. C. Fields

Rum Swizzle

SERVES 1 | PREP 5 MINUTES

INGREDIENTS

ice cubes
1½ shots dark rum
1½ shots gold rum
2 shots pineapple juice
2 shots orange juice
1 shot grenadine
2 dashes of bitters
orange twist for garnish

METHOD

1. Fill a tall glass with crushed ice and add all the ingredients apart from the orange peel.

2. Mix with a long spoon, garnish with the orange twist and serve!

Bananarama

SERVES 1 | PREP 5 MINUTES

INGREDIENTS

2 shots white rum
1 shot lime juice
½ shot banana liqueur
½ shot almond syrup
ice cubes
fresh mint and a banana slice
for garnish

METHOD

1. In a cocktail shaker, shake together all the ingredients (except the garnishes), without ice.
2. Pour the cocktail into a glass filled with crushed ice.
3. Top with more crushed ice then garnish with mint and banana.

THERE ARE SOME SURPRISING
HEALTH BENEFITS OF RUM.

IT'S ANTISEPTIC – SO A RUM A DAY
REALLY CAN KEEP THE DOCTOR AWAY.

STUDIES SUGGEST THAT RUM CAN
ALLEVIATE THE SYMPTOMS OF
ARTHRITIS AND DEMENTIA.

SO DRINKING RUM =
YOUNGER BRAIN AND BODY!

Hot Buttered Rum

SERVES 1 | PREP 5-10 MINUTES

INGREDIENTS

10 g (½ oz) butter
1½ tsp brown sugar
3 cloves
2 shots dark rum
cinnamon stick for garnish

METHOD

1. In a small pan over a low heat, melt the butter and sugar together with the cloves.

2. Remove the pan from the heat and add the dark rum, stirring well.

3. Strain the mixture through a sieve into a heatproof mug or glass, adding hot water to taste.

4. Garnish with the cinnamon stick and serve!

Passion and Orange Tiki

SERVES 1 | PREP 5 MINUTES

INGREDIENTS

ice cubes
½ shot lime juice
2 shots white rum
2 shots dark rum
2 shots passion fruit juice
1 shot orange juice
1 tbsp sugar syrup
1 tbsp grenadine
orange slices for garnish

METHOD

1. Fill a cocktail shaker with ice and add all the ingredients (except the garnish). Shake until the outside becomes cold and frosty.

2. Strain the mixture into a glass and garnish with the orange slices.

THE POPULARITY OF RUM HAS
SURGED IN RECENT YEARS
DUE TO IT FEATURING IN
HOLLYWOOD FILMS SUCH AS
PIRATES OF THE CARIBBEAN.

YO-HO-HO, AND A BOTTLE OF RUM!

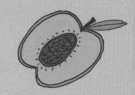

DRINKING RUM BEFORE
10AM MAKES YOU A PIRATE,
NOT AN ALCOHOLIC.

Earl Dibbles Jr.

Raspberry
Rum Mule

SERVES 1 | PREP 5 MINUTES

INGREDIENTS

ice cubes
2 shots rum
½ shot lime juice
1 tsp agave syrup (or honey)
5 raspberries, plus extra
for garnish
250 ml (8¾ fl oz) ginger beer
lime slices for garnish

METHOD

1. Fill an ice-filled cocktail shaker
   with the rum, lime juice, agave
   syrup and raspberries.
2. Shake until the outside becomes
   cold and frosty.
3. Strain the mixture into a glass
   half-filled with ice, then garnish
   with the additional raspberries
   and a couple of lime slices.

Salted Caramel Rum Float

SERVES 1 | PREP 5 MINUTES

INGREDIENTS

3 shots caramel sauce, plus
extra for garnish
1 tsp flaky sea salt
225 g (8 oz) pecan ice cream
2 shots dark rum
5 shots milk
whipped cream

METHOD

1. Pop all the ingredients in a
   blender and blend until smooth.

2. Pour into a glass, top with a
   generous helping of whipped
   cream and extra caramel sauce
   if you dare.

(You Make Me)
Coco Loco

SERVES 1 | PREP 5 MINUTES

INGREDIENTS

ice cubes
2 shots white rum
coconut water
lime wedges for garnish
mint sprig for garnish

METHOD

1. In a tall ice-filled glass, add the rum and top with coconut water to desired level.

2. Garnish with lime wedges and mint, then serve!

RUM WAS THE
WORLD'S FIRST EVER
SPIRIT, FIRST DISTILLED
IN THE CARIBBEAN
IN THE 1620s.

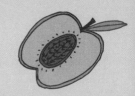

THERE WAS A SOUND IN
THEIR VOICES THAT
SUGGESTED RUM.

Robert Louis Stevenson

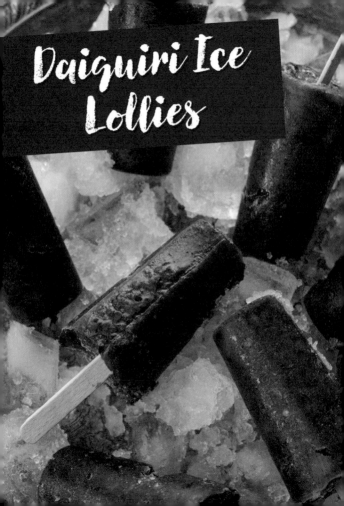

Daiquiri Ice Lollies

SERVES 4 | PREP 15 MINS + 4 HOURS

INGREDIENTS

150 g (5¼ oz) golden caster sugar
275 ml (9¼ fl oz) water
4 shots lime juice
4 shots white rum
150 g (5¼ oz) blackberries

METHOD

1. Stir the sugar and water in a pan over a low heat until dissolved.

2. Boil the mixture for approximately two minutes. Allow to cool, then add the lime juice and rum.

3. Purée then sieve ⅓ of the blackberries (keeping ⅔ aside).

4. Combine the purée and rum mix. Divide the whole blackberries then the rum purée between the lolly moulds and put a lolly stick in each.

5. Freeze for approximately four hours (or until firm) and serve.

Rum Boy Rum!

SERVES 1 | PREP 5 MINUTES

INGREDIENTS

ice cubes
1 shot mango purée
½ shot lime juice
½ shot grenadine
2 shots spiced rum
150 ml (5¼ fl oz) energy drink
lemon and lime slices for garnish
mint sprig for garnish

METHOD

1. In an ice-filled cocktail shaker, add the mango purée, lime juice, grenadine and rum. Put the lid on and shake until the outside is cold.

2. Add the energy drink to a glass and strain the mixture in the cocktail shaker on top.
   Garnish with the lemon and lime slices, and a sprig of mint.

AYE-AYE CAPTAIN DRINKING GAME
YO-HO-HO AND A SHOT OF RUM!

You will need:

A table
Enough shots of rum to fill the table

How to play:

The aim of the game is to not make 'aye' contact with your fellow drinkers.

All players stand around the table in a circle and close their eyes. One designated player shouts "aye-aye captain" and everyone opens their eyes in unison, staring at a particular player of their choice.

If any players are both staring at each other, they take a shot of rum out of the middle of the circle and lose a life. Each player has three lives and once they have lost all these lives they are out of the game (feel free to let everyone have more lives if you wish – that means more shots!).

The winner is the last person (or 2 people) standing and they are allowed to pick a forfeit for all the other players. Happy (and safe) drinking!

Long Island
Iced Tea

SERVES 1 | PREP 5 MINUTES

INGREDIENTS

ice cubes
½ shot vodka
½ shot gin
½ shot tequila
½ shot rum
½ shot triple sec
1 shot lime juice
5 shots cola
lemon slices for garnish

METHOD

1. In an ice-filled cocktail shaker, shake together all the ingredients (except the cola and lemon) until the outside of the shaker is cold and frosty.

2. Strain the mixture into an ice-filled glass, pour the cola on top and garnish with lemon slices.

Watermelon
Breeze

SERVES 2 | PREP 5 MINUTES (PLUS 1 HOUR FREEZING TIME)

INGREDIENTS

225 g (8 oz) watermelon, seeded and cubed, plus extra slices for garnish
5 shots rum (vanilla, coconut or pineapple)
1 tbsp honey
½ shot lime juice

METHOD

1. Freeze the watermelon cubes for one hour in a freezer.
2. Once frozen, add all the ingredients to a blender and blend until smooth.
3. Pour into two glasses, garnish with an unfrozen watermelon slice and serve!

NICKNAMES FOR RUM
INCLUDE 'AGUARDIENTE',
WHICH MEANS 'FIRE
WATER' IN SPANISH.

RUM IS TONIC THAT CLARIFIES
THE VISION, AND SETS THINGS
IN TRUE PERSPECTIVE.

Brian D'Ambrosio

Mai Tai

SERVES 1 | PREP 5 MINUTES

INGREDIENTS

ice cubes
2 shots white rum
½ shot triple sec
½ shot lime juice
2 shots pineapple juice
2 shots orange juice
dash of grenadine
1 shot dark rum
pineapple slice and maraschino
cherry for garnish

METHOD

1. Fill an ice-filled cocktail shaker
   with all the ingredients (except
   the garnishes), and shake well
   until the outside is cold and frosty.

2. Strain the mixture into an
   ice-filled cocktail glass and
   garnish with the pineapple
   slice and maraschino cherry.

Mince Pie Martini

SERVES 1 | PREP 5 MINUTES

INGREDIENTS

ice cubes
2 shots rum
1 tbsp mincemeat
1 shot apple juice
½ shot single cream
cinnamon powder for garnish

METHOD

1. Put the rum, mincemeat and apple juice into an ice-filled cocktail shaker and shake until the outside of the shaker is cold and frosty.

2. Strain the mixture into a glass and float the cream on top. Dust with cinnamon powder and serve!

Strawberries and Cream

SERVES 1 | PREP 10 MINUTES

INGREDIENTS

150 g (5¼ oz) strawberries,
halved, plus extra for garnish
2 shots rum
1 shot sugar syrup
1 shot peach schnapps
ice cubes
60 g (2 oz) whipped cream

METHOD

1. In a blender, pulse together the strawberries, rum, sugar syrup, peach schnapps and a large handful of ice cubes until smooth.

2. Pour ⅓ of the mixture into a tall glass then put a spoonful of the whipped cream on top. Repeat until the glass is full, garnish with strawberries, then serve!

Feelin' Peachy

SERVES 1 | PREP 5 MINUTES

INGREDIENTS

½ medium peach, chopped, plus
extra for garnish
3 cherries, pitted and stemmed
½ shot sugar syrup
½ shot lime juice
2 shots white rum

METHOD

1. In the bottom of a cocktail shaker,
   muddle together the chopped
   peach and cherries.

2. Add the rest of the ingredients
   (except the garnish) and shake
   until the outside of the shaker
   becomes cold and frosty.

3. Double strain the mixture into
   a glass and garnish with the
   peach slice.

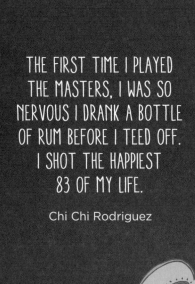

THE FIRST TIME I PLAYED
THE MASTERS, I WAS SO
NERVOUS I DRANK A BOTTLE
OF RUM BEFORE I TEED OFF.
I SHOT THE HAPPIEST
83 OF MY LIFE.

Chi Chi Rodriguez

THERE'S NAUGHT,
NO DOUBT,
SO MUCH THE SPIRIT
CALMS AS RUM.

Lord Byron

Rum Mocha

SERVES 1 | PREP 10 MINUTES

INGREDIENTS

4 shots milk
3 tbsp cocoa powder
2 tbsp sugar
1 shot espresso
1 shot dark rum
marshmallows for garnish

METHOD

1. In a small pan over medium heat, warm the milk, then whisk in the cocoa powder and sugar until smooth.
2. Add the espresso and rum, stir until combined and take the pan off the heat.
3. Pour the mixture into a mug and scatter over marshmallows.

A PIRATE'S LIFE FOR ME!

Many long-haul sailing missions to the Americas had issues with stagnant drinking water, so the water was mixed with rum and lime to create 'grog'. This was a safer alternative than plain water and was drunk liberally by pirates. The addition of citrus also helped to prevent scurvy!

Due to pirate ships being run under less control and formality than military or merchant ships, pirates often had full disregard for sobriety, meaning they were easily overtaken, as the crew were too drunk to fight or defend themselves!

Dark 'n' Stormy

SERVES 1 | PREP 5 MINUTES

INGREDIENTS

ice cubes
2 shots dark rum
3 shots ginger beer
½ shot lime juice
lime wedge for garnish

METHOD

1. Fill a tall glass with ice and add the rum.

2. Layer the ginger beer and lime juice on top of the rum and garnish with a lime wedge.

Thai Basil Daiquiri

SERVES 1 | PREP 5 MINUTES

INGREDIENTS

5 Thai basil leaves
2 shots sugar syrup
1 shot lime juice
2 shots white rum
pinch of salt
ice cubes

METHOD

1. Blend all the ingredients together in a blender until smooth.

2. In an ice-filled cocktail shaker, shake together all the ingredients until the outside of the shaker is cold and frosty.

3. Double strain the mixture into a glass and serve!

IF I EVER GO MISSING, PLEASE
PUT MY PHOTO ON A RUM BOTTLE,
NOT A MILK CARTON. I WANT
MY FRIENDS TO KNOW I AM MISSING!

Laurie Manzer

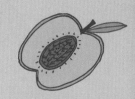

THE BEST IDEAS COME
WHILE SIPPING RUM.

Pavol Kazimir

Blue
Hawaiian

SERVES 1 | PREP 5 MINUTES

INGREDIENTS

ice cubes
2 shots white rum
2 shots blue curaçao
1 tsp coconut cream
4 shots pineapple juice

METHOD

1. Add all the ingredients to an
   ice-filled cocktail shaker.
   Put on the lid and shake until
   the outside is cold and frosty.

2. Strain into an ice-filled glass
   and serve!

RUM RECORDS

The largest glass of mojito recorded was 3,519 litres. It was made in 2016 by 4-Jack's Bar and Bistro in Punta Cana, Dominican Republic. It consisted of 700 litres of rum, 300 litres of lime juice, 700 litres of soda, 227 kg of sugar and 68 kg of mint!

I'm literally just having one ...

The oldest existing rum is
The Harewood Rum 1780. In 2011,
fifty-nine bottles of the rum were
discovered in the cellar of
Harewood House in Leeds, UK.

Party back at ours anyone?

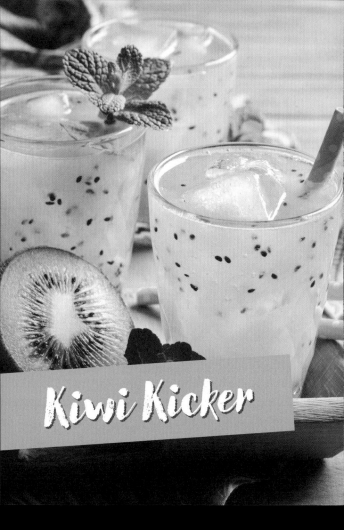

Kiwi Kicker

SERVES 1 | PREP 5 MINUTES

INGREDIENTS

4 shots kiwi purée
2 shots white rum
2 shots sugar syrup
1 shot lemon juice
ice cubes
sparkling water
mint sprig for garnish

METHOD

1. In a glass, stir together the kiwi purée, rum, sugar syrup and lemon juice.
2. Add ice and top with sparkling water. Garnish with mint and enjoy!

The Milkman

SERVES 1 | PREP 5 MINUTES

INGREDIENTS

2 shots whisky
½ shot dark rum
½ shot vanilla syrup
3 shots milk
ice cubes
cinnamon powder for garnish

METHOD

1. In an ice-filled cocktail shaker, add all the ingredients (except the garnish), put the lid on and shake until the outside is cold and frosty.

2. Strain into a glass and add ice. Sprinkle over some cinnamon powder and serve!

I WANT SOMEONE
TO LOOK AT ME THE WAY
I LOOK AT RUM.

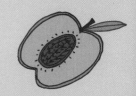

I LIVED ON RUM, I TELL YOU.
IT'S BEEN MEAT AND DRINK,
AND MAN AND WIFE, TO ME.

Robert Louis Stevenson

Rosemary Orange Cooler

SERVES 1 | PREP 10 MINUTES

INGREDIENTS

1 tsp sugar
½ tangerine, chopped
2 rosemary sprigs (1 for garnish)
2 shots white rum
ice cubes
½ shot free-range egg white, whipped
dried orange wheel for garnish

METHOD

1. Put the sugar in a bowl and gently coat the tangerine pieces in it.

2. Heat a small pan on high heat. Add one rosemary sprig and the tangerine, cooking until they caramelise (around two minutes).

3. Discard the rosemary and muddle the caramelised tangerine in the bottom of a glass, then stir in the rum and some ice.

4. Garnish with a rosemary sprig, the egg foam and dried orange slice.

Spiced
Rum Sour

SERVES 1 | PREP 5 MINUTES

INGREDIENTS

2 shots spiced rum
3 shots sour mix
½ shot ginger syrup
1 tsp turmeric
ice cubes
mint sprig and orange slices
for garnish

METHOD

1. In a cocktail shaker, add all the ingredients (except the garnishes), put on the lid and shake.

2. Add ice and shake again until the outside of the shaker is cold and frosty.

3. Strain the mixture into an ice-filled glass, then garnish with the mint and orange slices.

Jelly Shots

SERVES 1 | PREP 15 MINUTES (PLUS 2 HOURS CHILLING TIME)

INGREDIENTS

1 box jelly mixture (ideally pineapple or mango)
225 ml (8 fl oz) boiling water
5 shots coconut rum
125 ml (4½ fl oz) cold water

METHOD

1. In a medium bowl, mix together the jelly mixture and the boiling water, until dissolved.

2. Stir in the rum and cold water until combined.

3. Pour the mixture into shot glasses until ¾ full and refrigerate for two hours, until set.

Black Velvet

SERVES 1 | PREP 5 MINUTES

INGREDIENTS

ice cubes
1 shot black sesame syrup
2 shots dark rum
1 shot lime juice
orange twist for garnish

METHOD

1. In an ice-filled cocktail shaker, add all the ingredients (except the orange peel). Put on the lid and shake until the outside is cold and frosty.

2. Double strain the mixture into a coupe glass and garnish with an orange twist.

Forecast Hurricane

SERVES 1 | PREP 5 MINUTES

INGREDIENTS

ice cubes
2 shots white rum
2 shots dark rum
2 shots passion fruit juice
1 shot orange juice
½ shot grenadine
½ shot sugar syrup
½ shot lime juice
orange wheel for garnish
maraschino cherry for garnish

METHOD

1. Add all the ingredients (except the garnish) to an ice-filled cocktail shaker and shake until the outside is cold and frosty.

2. Strain the cocktail into a hurricane glass, then garnish with an orange wheel and cherry. Serve and enjoy!

Champagne Mojito

SERVES 1 | PREP 5 MINUTES

INGREDIENTS

ice cubes
small handful of mint leaves
1 shot rum
½ shot lime juice
1 tsp sugar syrup
dash of bitters
Champagne

METHOD

1. Put some ice and the mint leaves into the bottom of a wine glass.

2. Pour over the rum, lime juice, sugar syrup and bitters, then gently mix.

3. Top with Champagne to desired amount and sip away!

I SPEND HALF MY LIFE WONDERING IF
IT'S TOO LATE TO DRINK COFFEE
AND THE OTHER HALF WONDERING IF
IT'S TOO EARLY TO DRINK RUM.

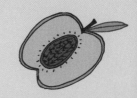

OH, YOU SAID RUN?

I THOUGHT YOU SAID RUM.

MANY PIRATES STARTED OFF
AS MILITARY SAILORS, BUT
SWITCHED TO PIRATING DUE TO THE
APPEALING LIFESTYLE, INCLUDING THE
LACK OF DRINKING RULES.

WHERE DO I SIGN UP?

RUM WAS READILY AVAILABLE IN
THE CARIBBEAN, SO PIRATES HAD
EASY ACCESS TO IT. THEY WOULD
LOOT SHIPS EXPORTING RUM,
THEN SELL IT AT PORTS.

HOWEVER, MORE OFTEN THAN NOT,
THE PIRATES WOULD DRINK ALL
THE RUM THEMSELVES!

Extra Spicy Daiquiri

SERVES 1 | PREP 5 MINUTES

INGREDIENTS

1 shot rum
1 shot Ancho Reyes Verde® (green chilli liqueur)
1 shot lime juice
½ shot sugar syrup
ice cubes
mint sprig for garnish
lime wheel for garnish

METHOD

1. Add the rum, Ancho Reyes Verde®, lime juice and sugar syrup to an ice-filled cocktail shaker and shake until the outside is cold and frosty.

2. Strain the mixture into a martini glass, then garnish with a mint sprig and lime wheel.

Grapefruit
Mojito

SERVES 1 | PREP 5 MINUTES

INGREDIENTS

1 tsp sugar
1 tsp lime juice
juice of ½ grapefruit
18 g (¾ oz) golden caster sugar
1 shot white rum
ice cubes
2 shots soda water
lime wedges for garnish

METHOD

1. Sugar rim your glass by dipping
   the rim of the glass in a little lime
   juice and sugar.

2. In the glass, crush together the
   grapefruit juice and sugar.
   Add the rum and mix well.

3. Fill the glass with ice and top
   with soda water. Garnish with
   lime wedges.

Pink Summer Cooler

SERVES 1 | PREP 5 MINUTES

INGREDIENTS

2 shots white rum
1 shot cranberry juice
ice cubes
125 ml (4½ fl oz) lemon soda
lemon wheel for garnish

METHOD

1. Pour the rum and cranberry juice into a glass and stir together.
2. Fill the glass with ice and top with lemon soda. Garnish with a lemon wheel and enjoy – summer in a glass!

Cranberry Prosecco Fizz

SERVES 1 | PREP 5 MINUTES

INGREDIENTS

2 shots white rum
½ shot lime juice
1 shot cranberry juice
2 shots prosecco

METHOD

1. Pour the rum, lime juice and cranberry juice into a prosecco glass.

2. Top with prosecco and enjoy!

WHY LOOK SO GLUM WHEN
DOCTOR RUM IS WAITING
FOR TO CURE YOU?

Oliver Herford

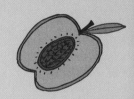

AUGUST IS NATIONAL RUM
MONTH, AND AUGUST 16TH
IS NATIONAL RUM DAY.

SO NOW YOU KNOW WHEN
TO BOOK TIME OFF WORK.

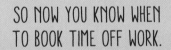

Cable Car

SERVES 1 | PREP 5 MINUTES

INGREDIENTS

1 tsp orange juice
1 tsp brown sugar
ice cubes
2 shots spiced rum
1 shot triple sec
½ shot free-range egg white
½ shot lemon juice
½ shot sugar syrup
orange twist for garnish

METHOD

1. Sugar rim your martini glass by dipping the rim in orange juice then brown sugar.

2. Add all the ingredients (except the orange twist) to an ice-filled cocktail shaker and shake until the outside is cold and frosty.

3. Strain the mixture into a martini glass and garnish with the orange twist.

Chai Toddy

SERVES 1 | PREP 10 MINUTES

INGREDIENTS

1 shot spiced rum
1 dash peppermint schnapps
½ shot runny honey
mug of tea (hot)
lemon wheel for garnish

METHOD

1. Pour the rum, schnapps and runny honey into a heatproof glass and stir together.
2. Top up with tea and garnish with a lemon wheel. Enjoy!

Photo Credits